If you are longing for a walk on the beach during the pandemic closures we are experiencing, read John Sweeder's book, Untethered Balloons, and his poetry will take you there. With a keen eye for detail and a deep appreciation of the ubiquitous phrase "down the shore," Sweeder captures life on the beach or boating on the bay with rich imagery and highly concentrated language. This wide-ranging collection also shines a light on other subjects, from city life, as in the tender childhood memories expressed in "Philly Boys," to nostalgic holiday reveries at work in "Show n' Tell," and sensitive forays into the complexities of life and loss, as in "The Mathematics of Faith," all in a mix of forms from free verse to the villanelle and pantoum, haiku and haibun, for a revelatory sensory journey.

—by Antoinette Libro,
Ph.D., award-winning poet, editor, and arts consultant

From the opening poems which pull readers gently into the vibrant world of a beloved seaside town, to the closing poems which tenderly reflect on life and death and what constitutes meaning for a person's existence, this book is a celebration of the human experience. Readers will find a kindred spirit in John Sweeder.

—Marya Parral,
poet and lead facilitator of the Jersey Cape Writers

It is not surprising that John Sweeder excels in both poetry and memoir. With an educator's keen observation of detail, and an outdoorsman's ability to capture the mental picture it creates in the moment, he has crafted a poetic journal of his lifetime. In his first collection, *Untethered Balloons: Poems,* Sweeder explores themes as diverse as seashore impressions and Christmas, school days and retirement, faith and death. With a generous use of the language and a particular talent for alliteration and metaphor, Sweeder packages his messages in a variety of forms, including haiku, prose poem and villanelle. If John Sweeder's life adds up to [nothing] more than words, the gift he has shared with lovers of words is considerable.

—Eva Feeley,
Survivors of Snake Bites

Untethered Balloons: Poems is a delightful collection of poetry drawn from the imagination of a life well-lived. Through deep reflection, clever wordsmithing and a sense of nostalgia, the poet offers vivid renderings of his personal experiences that provide insight and evoke a wide range of emotions. Prepare for a colorful journey that will leave you feeling…untethered.

—Maria Taney,
member of the Jersey Cape Writers

UNTETHERED BALLOONS

Untethered Balloons

A collection of poems

by

JOHN SWEEDER

Adelaide Books
New York / Lisbon
2021

UNTETHERED BALLOONS
A collection of poems
By John Sweeder

Copyright © by John Sweeder
Cover design © 2021 Adelaide Books

Published by Adelaide Books, New York / Lisbon
adelaidebooks.org

Editor-in-Chief
Stevan V. Nikolic

All rights reserved. No part of this book may be reproduced in any manner whatsoever without written permission from the author except in the case of brief quotations embodied in critical articles and reviews.

For any information, please address Adelaide Books
at info@adelaidebooks.org
or write to:
Adelaide Books
244 Fifth Ave. Suite D27
New York, NY, 10001

ISBN: 978-1-954351-92-9

Printed in the United States of America

for my loving wife, Bonnie
for my family and friends
and for those like me who, at one point or another in our lives,
have felt like untethered balloons

Contents

ONE

    The Drifters[7]   *17*

    Adolescent Heat   *18*

    Sand Surfers   *20*

    Wonderwheel Dreams[1]   *21*

    Driftwood   *23*

    Flat Fish   *25*

    The Jersey Angel   *26*

    Blues Busker[7]   *27*

    Floating in Place[2]   *29*

    The Birder[9]   *30*

    Drifting Eels   *31*

    Wounded Knee   *33*

    Before and Beyond   *35*

    Scarcely Hooked   *36*

    Chicken Bone Beach: Circa 1949   *37*

TWO

    Philly Boys *41*

    Infatuated Corridors *42*

    February 9th, 1964 in Black and White *43*

    Alien Homecoming *44*

    Barbara *45*

    Sister Collette[1] *46*

    Love and War on Campus in the Spring of 1968 *47*

    America's Wound Dresser *49*

    Lunch at Restaurant Kapitanova Kuca in Mali Ston *50*

    We Look *51*

THREE

    Perishing Twice[1] *55*

    Island Produce *56*

    He Writes with his Actions[10] *57*

    I Bumped into a Poem *58*

    Child Artist[1] *60*

FOUR

    Smell-fish Dinner *63*

    Ode to Key West *64*

    Gumbo *65*

Breakfast Philly Style *66*

Tony's Take-out Pizza *67*

The Flortician *68*

FIVE

sudden buds appear[3] *71*

creamy white fungi *72*

yellow swallowtail *73*

wild backyard mint leaf [3] *74*

SIX

Beach-town Christmas[11] *77*

Jersey-Cape Christmas Contemplation *78*

At Christmastime *79*

Lionel Reveries *80*

A 50's Christmas Eve *81*

Christmas Boys 1957 *83*

Magi *84*

Holly Trees *85*

Show n' Tell *86*

SEVEN

Septal Defects[1] *89*

undocumented immigrant[4] *91*

A Venezuelan Mother's Plight *92*

Touch-Screen Viruses[1] *93*

No Relief *94*

Drones[5] *96*

white noise *97*

Closet Space *99*

Contextual *101*

May-Day Mayflies[1] *102*

Gothic Dreams[1] *103*

presidential candidate[1] *104*

Trinculo's Insight[1] *106*

EIGHT

Faith[8] *109*

Fortune of War *110*

Give Me Retirement *111*

Light and Dark at the Cineplex[6] *112*

Apparitions and Relics *114*

Winter's Clean-up *116*

Our Father *118*

Melanoma *120*

His Ashes[6] *121*

The Mathematics of Faith[1] *123*

Acknowledgements **125**

[1] *originally appeared in an issue of Opening Line Literary 'Zine*
[2] *originally appeared in an issue of the Ocean City Sentinel*
[3] *originally appeared in an issue of the Haiku Journal*
[4] *originally appeared in an issue of the Burningword Literary Journal*
[5] *originally appeared in an issue of Shantih Journal*
[6] *originally appeared in an issue of the Adelaide Literary Magazine*
[7] *originally appeared in the Adelaide Literary Award 2018 Poetry Anthology*
[8] *originally appeared in Ancient Paths Online*
[9] *originally appeared in River Poets Journal*
[10] *originally appeared in The 2016 Poetry Marathon Anthology*
[11] *originally appeared in the Ocean City Sentinel and then the Cape May County Herald*

List of Credits for Poems Previously Published **127**

About the Author **131**

ONE

The Drifters

Mid-autumn mornings just after a fierce
coastal storm, I walk along a quiet beach
scavenging for pitted shards of sea-glass
with their frosted greens and ambers;
for sea-shells, those exoskeletons of scallops
and clams; for curvilinear whelk
egg cases—Nature's Slinkys.

I overturn a horseshoe crab and finger
a black shark's tooth. I hoist an ashen conch
shell to my ear and listen for the sound
of the crashing ocean surf. I spot pieces
of gray weathered pine and wonder whether
they have wandered from a boat dock
or washed up from under the boardwalk.

I pursue these peripatetic ocean remnants
to remind myself of my sandy childhood treks
along the more crowded summer beach
where, amid the drifting sounds of carousels
and roller coasters, and smells of crab cakes
and curly fries, my nature walks came and went
more quickly than I had wished they had.

Adolescent Heat

Remember

the first time we stayed up all night
to watch the red sun rise over the ocean

the addictive adolescent heat we felt
on that Friday night down the shore in mid-July

Remember

how we all chipped in to rent a room
for the weekend in that shabby Victorian hotel

those well-worn wooden steps, the smell of mildew,
the peeling paint, the funnel-shaped ceiling, the torn shade

Remember

not unpacking anything except the bathing suits
and bottles of lime vodka we smuggled in our duffle bags

buying those cheap fish-cake dinners and taking them
back to our room to scarf down with free tartar sauce

Remember

walking the boards barefooted until closing time
and then sneaking down to the ocean's edge until we got chased

pacing deserted 3 AM back-street sidewalks (still barefooted)
the surprising coolness and humidity assailing our skin

Remember

how the amber traffic lights and neon shop-front signs blinked
and stared at us as we waited impatiently for the pre-dawn light

asking one another *what time does the beach open* so we could
lay down on the soft sand, fall asleep, and nurture our sunburns

Remember

waking up thirsting for a frosty Coke, aching for a chance to meet
one of the tight bodies that cruised the wet sand in the
    afternoon sun

being born again: touching a lit match, scraping a knee, balancing
ourselves on a two-wheeler for the second wonderful time in
    our lives

Sand Surfers

Little boys and girls don slick black wet suits
as they practice surfing on ocean-edge
sand. Arms outstretched like seagull wings, they balance
their sun-screened bodies on un-waxed surfboards
while nearby parents dutifully watch the
fledglings from beneath their rented yellow-
and-green-striped beach chairs and umbrellas. Older
kids who sea-surf with confidence wonder
when their nestling understudies will leave
the safety of the unwavering silt
and venture into deep ocean waters
to feel the thrilling thrust of undulant
waves, cloaked currents, and sea-born independence.

Wonderwheel Dreams

Old folk and kids dream of parallelogram
    shadows cast by the sun's rays past metal
        railings onto gray boardwalk planks. It is
            early summer: school has let out; snowbirds

returned from their tropical Southern climes.
    On aqua and carrot coaster bikes they
        glide along the boards with chrome-spoked wheels,
            longing to glimpse freshly-planted dune grasses,

those green-golden sentries that protect their
    isle from ocean floods. Zigzagging between
        white parallel-line bike lanes, they spot the
            solitary jetty angler clutch his surf rod

like a medieval knight with lance in hand.
    They ride past scores of rectangular benches
        coated with pastel hues, inscribed with plaques
            bequeathed by aboriginals to honor lost loved ones;

past the chevron-shaped trail of the wary
    red fox, bespeckling the sand with linear
        tracks that disappear into dune dens 'neath
            beach plum shrubbery and cusped yuccas;

John Sweeder

past cedar rail posts that guide beachgoers
    through tall dunes to wet sand and saltwater;
        past bikers' oases: pyramidal pavilions providing
            caesuras, shade, and cool ocean breezes.

Old folk and kids dream of parallelogram
    shadows—Wonderwheels of geometric dreams

Driftwood

Have you ever noticed
the lone beachcomber
who, like a piece of driftwood,

pitches a tattered tent beside
the boardwalk for a week
or two then suddenly leaves?

Whenever I do, I peek to see
if anyone's camped inside.
Usually I find the canvas empty

except for a torn blanket
or soppy paper bag
or pair of spiritless sneakers.

I wonder if the absentee
is young…estranged…addicted,
imagining what it'd be like

if I were a seashore wanderer.
Some local denizens treasure pieces
of driftwood they find on the beach

and turn them into art: a turtle,
a seahorse—perhaps a sandpiper.
Others treat driftwood

John Sweeder

as indifferently as Nature,
waiting for the next storm
or flood tide to raft them out.

Flat Fish

As I peer up at his boat, *Caliban*,
through the warming late spring waters of this
New Jersey back bay, I see his lucent
line descend. His chartreuse jig bumps along
bottom mussel beds as he persuades me
to lunch with him. The immortal current
slows as high tide approaches. He thinks I swim
in unfamiliar waters, but not so:
I have slipped along these bottom sands
through its cuts and channels for centuries,
surviving Nor'easters, waterspouts,
predators—and Shakespearean tempests.

The Jersey Angel

It lives near tidal estuaries
near rich salt-marsh earth
in touch with wind and cedar creeks
where skimmers and sanderlings feed.

Near rich salt-marsh earth
with its currents, crabs, and minnows
skimmers and sanderlings feed
in touch with wind and cedar creeks.

With its currents, crabs, and minnows
a regenerative pineland thrives
in touch with wind and cedar creeks
and lighting and fire

a regenerative pineland thrives
then dies then lives again
because of lighting and fire.
It lives near tidal estuaries.

Blues Busker

The young man
cradles his harmonica
with cupped hands
caressing it with his soul,
coaxing emotion
from its compact form
as poets do with pens.

Tunes jazz from
his mouth harp
through long fingers
with knobby knuckles,
wafting tabasco tunes
as spicy as
red beans and rice.

From street-side curbs
he plays his
rhymes and rhythms
as we tap toes
on tourist sidewalks,
listening to his free verse
rise to the heavens.

His blues drift skyward
like invisible scores

John Sweeder

bestowing sharps and flats
that we store
for safekeeping
and later retrieve from
our mind's music box.

Floating in Place

Gulls float in place buttressed by the same wind
that blows down on us with cheeky harshness
as we cross our back-bay bridge determined
to view the winged fauna and lush marshes.
In late winter, gulls grow scarce in number
as do tourists who walk along the strand,
but we robust few who knuckle under
find wonders as we trek along the span:
red-billed oyster catcher, tern-like skimmer,
clapper rail, laughing gull, snowy egret—
arriving each spring near the shimmering
saltwater's edge—building nests.
We bikers and birders all float in place
not unlike bridge birds competing for space.

The Birder

A lone colonial home perches along
the Delaware River on fertile farmland
lying opposite Hessian Trenton where
one winter long ago General Washington's
troops crossed ice-cold waters in open boats.
Peering through its crown-glass windowpanes
it spies pairs of Canada geese splashing
gawkily into frigid early-spring
waters watching them paddle towards shore
fighting swift currents with webbed feet
that oscillate swiftly like soldiers' oars
battling nature's ruthless elements
all to create sheltered nests on grassy
banks for their legacy gosling offspring.

Drifting Eels

Upon a new-moon midnight,
as high-tide ebbs
I carry rod, reel, and eels
to an ocean esplanade
to fish for stripers.

Wild waves curl and crash
under the boardwalk
where bass wallop
smaller baitfish and snack
on cracked-open clams.

I cast a slippery snake
into the saltwater
boarder where
boardwalk lamplight
meets ocean darkness.

The eel drifts and wriggles
on a weightless hook
in the ocean current
unaware that
its predator is my prey.

Triggered by movement
shadow and scent, a bass

John Sweeder

stuns, then swallows the bait.
The hook is set
and the reel screams.

Like the unwitting eel
I often swim in dangerous
waters, twisting and turning
to shake loose
of life's tethers.

Adapting to survive
I bury my head in the sand,
or scream like a reel,
or just play dead
to avoid being swallowed.

Wounded Knee

As morning clouds turn red at dawn, the sky
softly socializes with the dense salt
air. Meg unties her boat's stern and bow lines,
starts the outboard engine and leaves the dock,
making sure to skirt the fluky sand bar
that hides just underneath the water's skin.

It's July and Meg's wrinkled swarthy skin
sheds small beads of sweat. She stares at the sky
weighing if she'll wear a jacket to bar
any precipitous shower or salt
water from breaching her dry clothes. Docking
her skiff's speed Meg motors in a straight line

heading for red and green buoys that line
her boat up with deep channel waters. *Skin
So Soft* keeps biting bugs at bay. Meg docks
her original plans, given the sky's
foreboding blush, and opts instead to salt
her trek with a stop at a local bar

after her morning's crabbing trip (barring
any mishaps). She sets baited trot lines
and waits for blue crabs to grab the salted
alewives. As she retrieves her prey, Meg skins
her knee. She damns last night's full moon—the sky's
bewitching sign—and heads back to the dock.

John Sweeder

Nestling her boat into its slip, the dock
shivers slightly then stabilizes. Bars
of light peek through anvil clouds in the sky.
A storm's emanant. Tightening boat lines
with steadfast tugs, Meg assesses her skinned
knee and decides to cleanse the wound with salt

water. She alights, hoisting the salty
crustaceans she has caught onto the dock.
After spitting three times, Meg curtly skins
herself for her carelessness. Then, barring
her earlier plans, she makes a bee line
for *Joe's* to breakfast 'neath the squally sky.

Sibylline skies sometimes dumbfound old salts
who unwittingly slip on lines and docks
like bars of wet soap slimy as eel skins.

Before and Beyond

Just before darkness
you hear bashful baitfish slap the back-bay's
top-water. Alone, you cast your floating plug
over and past liquid concentric circles,
translucent bullseyes built by wary schools
of peanut bunker. Your lure twitches like
a crippled cricket atop the water's surface
then vanishes as suddenly as an ace of spades
from a magician's hand. Feeling the stunning
power of the predator's punch you raise
your rod tip, setting the hook. Time evaporates
with combat's uncertain outcome.
You imagine guiding the game fish to your net,
removing the lure, releasing your trophy
to its rightful real estate—the waters that lay
just beyond darkness.

Scarcely Hooked

Shad fishing is a shrewd trade-off between
handling and manhandling
    from John McPhee's *The Founding Fish*

Spawning buck and roe shad return each spring
to cold swollen rivers. Expert anglers
affix darts and spoons to pellucid lines
casting them up-current to magnetize

and induce fasting, fleet, flashes of light.
They strike, skewer themselves, swim cross current,
rise, and tail-walk across riffles, shaking
their heads like intractable youngsters who

shun being led by lips. Schooled together
they climb ladders, rest in pools, and enter
precarious narrows. Shrewd rod handlers
land most of their catch. Manhandlers do not.

For it's between nature and nurturing
they discover they are both scarcely hooked.

Chicken Bone Beach: Circa 1949

Ya says ya rememba gettin on da
train to 'Lantic City? Well I do too.
I sitten in da back with *da Negro
Green Book* 'tween m' knees, read'n 'bout Chicken
Bone Beach. Damn, I says to m'self, dis gonna
be fun. I gets to swim in da ocean, eats
m' cold fried chicken on da hot sand beach,
rub elbows with da likes of Sammy Davis
n' Duke Ellington, n' maybe, just maybe
sidle up right next to a couple of
dem Harlem showgirls. Mmm-mm. I'm so lookin'
forward to dat.
                I also remembas
dis other time dis fine-looking colored man sits
down right across from me. Tells me dat he's
goin' to Chicken Bone Beach too. I ax him,
What you do for livin'? He's says he's a
pro-fes-sion-al pho-tog-ro-pher, ya'know
a pitcher-taker.
                What dat you say? You gonna
take my pitcher on d'beach? Gonna make me
famous in *Color Magazine*? Gonna
get Champaign Charlie to give me a glass
of his finest? Well, count me in.
                      What you
say you name was? Mr. John dooba Mosely?

John Sweeder

Well, it's mighty nice to meet cha' sir.
Mighty nice indeed.
                    Ya sees I'm on m'way
to 'Lantic City ta meet my cousin, n'
right afta church we gonna go back to
our Northside crib, get a change of clothes,
n' head down Missouri Avenue with
our picnic baskets. Does y'all like collard
greens? My cousin makes da best.
                          Well, what you
know? Here we are. We's arrived. You take care
now. I'll sees you on the beach. Don't forget
ya cam'ra. I won't forget da beer

TWO

Philly Boys

We Philly boys remember well the concrete driveway we once called "The Alley," which separated parallel blocks of two-story red-brick row homes. A pair of tall cedar telephone poles at each end of The Alley watched over us like sentries as we threw small white pimple balls at their thick black lines which stretched from one side of the driveway to the other; we Philly boys who wore our canvas high-top Chuck Taylors proudly; we Philly boys who played impromptu games like half-ball, wire-ball, and chink; we Philly boys who, all summer long, flipped Topps baseball cards and watched them tumble to the ground as softly as whirlybirds landed on tarmacs; we Philly boys who played knee-football each autumn on small patches of crab grass riddled with dandelion seedpods; we Philly boys who fought over "safes" and "outs" and "foul balls" as we ran bases made from old rags and worn-out caps; we Philly boys who tossed brown-rubber basketballs at green plywood backboards with orange metal rims that our dads built for us to "keep us busy and out of trouble"; we Philly boys who laughed until our ribs and stomachs ached and our eyes watered as we swallowed mouthfuls of Heinz Catsup and let them intermingle with our saliva to mimic the blood we sucked from the necks of our imaginary female victims, that foul-smelling blood which trickled down from our mouths onto our chins; we Philly boys who seldom, if ever, hung out with girls.

facebook
soccer moms—
girls no longer left behind

Infatuated Corridors

Sex-drives, like crocus bulbs, awake early
each spring in hallways of junior high schools.
Girls slip into hot-pink shorts and skimpy
white tees in goose-bump weather exposing
breasts and thighs to their shorter boyfriends and
taller girlfriends. Guys reveal plaid boxer
tops and fresh haircuts displaying tresses
of rainbow highlights and oblique angles,
attracting unwanted teacher stares. Teens
camber against khaki lockers dawdling
between bells, forgetting weighty textbooks.
Walking arms-around-waists in corridors,
couples part with such sweet sorrow as they
enter their biology and English
and history and algebra classes.

February 9th, 1964 in Black and White

It's Sunday night and I just get back from
walkin' my dog, Freckles, down by the vacant
lot at the end of our street so I can
catch a smoke without my mom knowin,' and
I see her watching *The Ed Sullivan
Show* on our 19-inch black-and-white Sylvania.
"Who are those guys?" I ask. "The Beatles," she says.
"What's up with those British accents?"
Not expectin' Mom to answer me, she says,
"They're singing, 'I Want to Hold Your Hand.'"
So, I start payin' closer attention
and see a young white girl in the
audience wearin' pointy black-and-white-
framed glasses screamin' like she was watchin'
Elvis. Some other girls have tears runnin' down their cheeks.
Mom asks me, "Who's your favorite Beatle?"
"How should I know? The drummer looks cool though."
"That's Ringo," she says.
How's she know his name? I' thinkin.'
She says, "He makes me smile."
I like his hair and how he shakes his head
from side to side as he smacks his cymbals.

So, I'm back at school next day and everyone's
talkin' about them–this group I never
heard of until last night–wonderin' if
they will ever play soul music.

Alien Homecoming

Remember that bike, that Strawberry Moon?
The silhouettes of the boy and ET?
We felt just like them that dark night in June.

Twin aliens alone in one cocoon,
we helped keep one another company.
Remember that bike, that Strawberry Moon?

We drifted in space, two untethered balloons
testing gravity, floating aimlessly.
We felt just like them that dark night in June.

But physics prevailed; our descent came soon
after: yours to the land, mine to the sea.
Remember that bike, that Strawberry Moon?

Falling to Earth, taking that opportune
time to find ourselves–our identity–
We felt just like them that dark night in June.

Understanding we'd no longer commune
the way we once did, we knew we were free.
Remember that bike, that Strawberry Moon?
We felt just like them that dark night in June.

Barbara

Barbara sat in the desk right in front of me during our first few years of elementary school, in the fourth row, seat number five, her dirty-blonde ponytail bobbing up and down mere inches from my nose, smelling of White Rain shampoo. How could I not give it a tug from time to time? (Her ponytail, not my nose, I mean.) One year, on Valentine's Day, our 3rd-grade teacher brought a record player into class and threw a party for us during morning recess. I asked Barbara if she would slow dance to Sam Cooke's "You Send Me." Neither of us knew how, so we took each other's hands and began swaying side to side, with enough space between our torsos to park a 58' Chevy. As Sam crooned the words, "Honest you do…" Barbara leaned in and whispered that she and her family were going to move away in June and that she would not be returning to our school next fall. I thanked her for letting me know, but I didn't mean it. I was mad—and sad. We returned to our desks and sat silently apart forever.

I opened Facebook on my computer this morning, saw the prompt "Find Friends" and thought of Barbara for the first time in decades wondering, "Whatever happened to her? Did she marry and have kids? Was she alive? I then remembered my wife and how both were alike in so many ways.

Sister Collette

She begins each school day with a prayer.
In the name of the Father, she utters,
head bowed, eyes down, her habit's hem gently
caressing the hoary oaken floorboards.

I sit in the last seat of the last row
where I belong. Sister never questions
my tardiness. She just makes eye contact.
I am grateful I do not have to lie.

She knows I smoke cigarettes at lunchtime;
I reek like rhinoceros piss. But since
I am an altar boy and point guard on
the school's varsity basketball team, she

pretends not to notice. I respect sister:
her sacrifices, her tolerance—
my idiocies, my egocentrism.
Perhaps I will become a schoolteacher.

Love and War on Campus in the Spring of 1968

I never ask, "Do you want to have sex?"
I just want to smoke a little grass
with you at midnight on the quad and play
"Penny Lane" on guitar as you listen
and I forget that I'm going to war
soon. You urge me not to cut my long hair.

"One of your best qualities is your hair,"
you say, "It makes you look very sexy."
The songs I strum help me forget the war,
the foreign bodies, lost classmates. The grass
we sit upon is alive like spring. "Listen,"
you say, "It's getting chilly. Can you play

a tune that will warm us up? Why not play
'Good Morning Starshine' from the stage show, *Hair*?"
As I sing "there's love in your skies" you listen
and smile and ask if I want to have sex
before the sun comes up. We smoke more grass,
caress, fall asleep. The Viet Nam War

seems as near as your love beads, yet the war
remains this far-off phantasm that plays
havoc with my unconsciousness. The grass's
faint effects wear off. I awake, my hair
sodden from parasomnia, our sex
postponed. It's almost dawn. You say, "Listen.

John Sweeder

Can you hear the chapel bells toll? Listen.
They're the sound of peace." You wipe the war
sweat from my forehead. My sexual
instincts repressed, replaced by fear, I play
one final song to douse my hairier
hallucinations and let them go to grass.

You sing, "To everything/ turn, turn," The grass,
now dry, sits up as if it's listening
to your verse. "There is a season…." My hair
is a protest like the hymn you pray. Wars
are tauten dramas, chronicled plays
about youth, love, song, outcry, death, and sex.

Some actors cut their hair and go off to wars;
some quitclaim for greener grass, not playing
the listening game; some find solace in sex.

America's Wound Dresser
(In honor of Walt Whitman)

I watch you watch youthful soldiers return
from battle fields to crowded hospitals.
You listen carefully to us and learn
about our suffering. You see brittle
limbs and punctured lungs nursed by wound dressers.
You smell the gangrene stench; hear unsuppressed
groans; but remain calm under pressure
as our blood drips onto your notebook desk.
Yet, as you see our nation devolving
into brutality, you look instead
to the stars, helping us rise, dissolving
our fears—staying close, just next to our beds.
You write our kin. You hug us. You kiss us.
You say there's a future ahead for us.

Lunch at Restaurant Kapitanova Kuca in Mali Ston

You don't believe me when I tell you that
one ingurgitates oysters through one's nose.

You smile. On this dry desert afternoon
owner Lidija Kralj sets our table

outdoors, beneath her pitched turquoise awning.
We eat our saline bivalves–six apiece

raw–facing the ghost-blue channel
that foregrounds a pewter mountain range.

In the shade we watch white wooden skiffs
crowd the rocky shoreline. Two tourist clouds

pass idly overhead. Lidija buses
our plates when we've finished. "I grill oysters,

a house specialty," she says with pride. So
we order twelve and split them as before.

Afterwards, I hold your salty fingertips
and watch a tear slip down your cheek and touch your lips.

We Look

Look, Jane, Look!
Look at this painting:
See the two neighborhood children making chalk talk
As they play hopscotch on a sidewalk.

Look, Dick, Look!
Look at that painting:
See the snow that Robert Frost saw long ago
The night his horse shook harness bells
in the deep New England woods.

Look, Jane, Look!
Look at this painting:
See the fish and turtles swim in their
mystical elliptical pattern,
Returning to their tentacled Hawaiian banyan tree.

Look, dick, Look!
Look at that painting:
See how the brush strokes become working boats
As they motor along the Maine coast?

Look, Jane, Look!
Look at this painting:
See the Venetian moon, ornate gaslight, and crescent gondola
Smile and wink at us as we spoon while
cruising The Grand Canal.

John Sweeder

Look, Dick, Look!
Look at that painting:
See the medieval city of Dubrovnik
with its red roofs, stone walls,
And harbor-side restaurants where we dined
on dinosauric, non-caloric prawns?

Look, Jane, Look!
Look at our gallery of paintings:
Each one a page in a scrapbook
reminding us where we've been
and what we've done since we first saw Spot run.

THREE

Perishing Twice

The aging poet's ice-chipped tongue
melted as he wrung
that apocalyptic verse from
between his frigid lips
pursed with blistering intent
in Fire and Ice:
Buffalo wings with blue cheese, or
boilermakers in frosty mugs?
Either would suffice.

Island Produce

In island solitude
the poet waits
for inspiration
like the dirt farmer
waits for rain during
a summer drought,
each knowing that
insight like growing
requires patience.

But when soaking
showers finally arrive
odic insights like
organic fruits and vegetables
replenish, their yields
savored one bite
at a time, no morsel
wasted.

He Writes with his Actions

He writes with his actions.
Rising from his bed each morning
he grabs his coffee before
confronting his computer screen.

Rising from his bed each morning
he remembers fragments of dreams.
Confronting his computer screen
he begins typing intuition.

Remembering fragments of dreams
he wakes up abruptly
and begins typing his intuition
so he does not forget.

I Bumped into a Poem

I bumped into a poem
and knocked it to the ground.
I thought I may have killed it—
at first, it made no sound.

I noticed it was breathing
tried to bring it to its feet
but I stumbled accidently
and kicked it back into the street.

Then I stepped onto a stanza
thought I broke one of its lines,
but it stretched like Turkish taffy
and began to sing and rhyme.

It crooned with such sweet rhythm
I danced and clapped in time,
and struck my shoe soles so hard
that their worn leather shined.

When the poem finished singing
I helped it to its feet,
took it home to my apartment
and fed it shredded wheat.

It went to bed right after
and didn't watch TV

but laid awake all night
versing to be free.

It yearned for inspiration
and woke me up at dawn
to beat me in a game of chess:
it made my king its pawn.

Smiling, the poem thanked me
and said, "It's time to go"
but before it did it made its bed
then paused to let me know

that the time we spent together
helped fertilize its muse
like a drummer, bass, and pianist
jam to improvise the blues.

I walked it to my entrance door
and said with words sincere
"I'll miss you. Please come again."
Then I watched it disappear.

Child Artist

With watercolors and brushes she paints
forlorn sea bass with worried school-bell eyes,
dolphins with underbites, shoebox flounder.
Her cerulean clam with red crooked
smile stares at me, but she does not. Only
her autistic portraits emote.

FOUR

Smell-fish Dinner

Young Kelsi goes crabbing with me every
August. She likes the smell of gasoline
fumes as we refuel our skiff, the salt air,
decomposed seaweed at low tide, and the
odor of onions that lace her lunch-time
submarine sandwich. She likes the sweet smell
of her Stewart's Root Beer and zesty scent
of my hoppy Bud. She insists that I
handle the slippery bunker that we
use for bait carping, "It stinks up my hands."

Afloat, hours pass quickly. Looking up
at anvil-gray clouds forming, I sense that
rain is coming. We return to the dock,
inhaling the aroma of chowder
clams from the near-by waterfront restaurant.

Back home I steam our catch in a big black
pot. We eat our crabs "dirty," cleaning each
one with our bare hands, removing grassy
intestines and cloudy lungs. Kelsi smiles
as she smells the cooked crabs seasoned with Old
Bay, licking rusty spices from her pink
fingertips, savoring each crescent claw,
each morsel of snow-white, back-fin crabmeat.
We consume every Sook and Jimmy.
Kelsi thanks me for her "smell-fish dinner."

Ode to Key West

Sunsets on sailboats
Cuban coffee at ten
Roosters on dirt roads
Fantasy friends

Slow turtle races
Lemon-lime houses
Back-yard palm trees
Colorful blouses

Eggs-Benedict breakfasts
Scubas and snorkels
Movie-star cat names
Tourists with smiles

Gumbo

I like my gumbo chickened
not pigged
not alligatored
not shrimped:
not what-evered

I like my gumbo chickened
stewed
not fried or poached
not sautéed or barbecued:
not how-evered

I like my gumbo chickened
in New Orleans
Nashville
or Charleston:
not where-evered

I like my gumbo chickened
morninged
nooned
or nighted:
when-evered

Breakfast Philly Style

Scrapple you greasy
gray brick of mush you sit still
on my white plate next to a
couple of fried eggs
and wait for me to eat you

Yo, Cuz! Pass me the catsup

Tony's Take-out Pizza

Tony's pepperoni grin
leaps over the countertop
onto the lid of the eponymous pizza box.

Resting in its cardboard coffin,
the hot pie sits beside me
beltless in my car's front seat.

Arriving home, I ravage it
as I watch the Friday-evening News
with my glass of Italian red.

The Flortician

He poisons ivy,
beheads petunias,
drowns cactus,
garrotes grasses,
prunes fingers,
mulches rocks,
and feeds weeds.

FIVE

sudden buds appear
on purple wisteria—
mysterious spring

creamy white fungi
grow on lone, leafless branches
of chaos-theory fig trees
in mid-April: spring weather
arrives late this year.

yellow swallowtail
jigs from blossom to blossom—
nature's Riverdance

wild backyard mint leaf
floats in glass of cold ice-tea—
ambrosial bliss

SIX

Beach-town Christmas

Shop owners reeve thin twine through Yuletide wreaths
of pine and holly, bejeweled with white night
lights and perched on street posts for a few brief

weeks. Locals listen to Bing Crosby's *White
Christmas* careen down carless down-town streets
through tinny, town-hall speakers. Traffic lights

blink at unabashed black-backed gulls who eat
discarded shards of saltwater taffy
dropped by tired toddlers. Fat Santas greet

elfin children. Winter winds blow chaffy
sand from nearby bay and beach, as shoppers
seek shelter in the mom-and-pop coffee
shop, or church with spires of green copper.

Jersey-Cape Christmas Contemplation

On a late December eve you watch
a scavenging red-tailed hawk
land in the sling-shot crotch
of a backyard pitch pine tree
competing with a local beach fox
for squirrel and rabbit prey.

You see rusty wrens and bloodshot cardinals
seeking sanctuary from avian predators
among the loblolly pines and red cedars
no longer able to hide among
the bony fingers of fig-tree branches
now exposed by early winter frost.

You think of the hillside shepherds of Judea
and, like them, marvel at how two poor
pilgrims, Mary and Joseph, survived
their Bethlehem quest, seeking shelter
for their sacred Infant on that holy
winter's eve long ago.

At Christmastime

At Christmastime my sister speaks to me
at odd moments: as I blow on hot tea,
swirl cinnamon sticks, or fetch the red tie
that hides in the back of my closet. I
don't resist her pedantry: she warns me
not to be overly melancholy
as I gift shop or trim our Yuletide tree.
Faithful Christian, her soft voice a latchkey
to a skeptical soul not fully free,
she retells aged tales that beatify
the world, just as the Christ Child did, that spry
bairn to whom Mary sung a lullaby.
Now gone many years, I still wonder why
at Christmastime my sister speaks to me.

Lionel Reveries

Not long ago, parents bought their children
model trains for Christmas. On December
mornings, just after they awoke, giddy
kids slid down bannisters as quickly as
they tore apart wrapping paper which cloaked
carrot cardboard boxes holding raven
steam engines that pulled coal-laden tenders,
radiant searchlight, crane and box cars, and
cardinal cabooses. Dads and moms taught
girls and boys to fashion straight and curved bits
of train track into voltaic figure
eights—magical infinities powering
locomotives spewing scented trails of
steam from miniature smoke stacks into
wee alcoves of childhood fantasies.

A 50's Christmas Eve

On Christmas Eve, as I
finish watching "I Love Lucy"
on our 12-inch black n' white Philco,
a candy-cane Santa
descends our staircase
and plops himself down
next to me, smiling
and jingling. (He jingles
cause he's got a green felt purse
full of shiny copper pennies
stashed away in his
big red pocket—a gift for me!)
He looks into my eyes
and holds my hand tenderly
like my Uncle Jack does.
I sit on his seat-cushion lap
distracted, with sideways eyes,
looking at you who stands
across the room holding
a Kodak Brownie belt high,
telling me to smile and say, "Cheese."
But I remain silent, uncertain,
thinking about what
I'm gonna ask Santa
for, for Christmas.
Suddenly, a flashbulb pops

John Sweeder

startling Santa and me
but not the hallowed
Nativity figures in the diorama
that rests atop our TV.

Christmas Boys 1957

December Sundays
little boys in wooden pews
dream of Christmas toys.
Monsignors preach from pulpits
about gifts from the Magi.

Red and blue Tonka
trucks carry water in tanks
load logs, dump refuse:
cargo as precious to them
as gold, frankincense, and myrrh.

Magi

Six footprints in snow
Left by three far-away kings—
Feel the manger's warmth

Holly Trees

Green leaves from holly trees
prick our fingertips as we prune
cold crooked branches
and fashion Yuletide wreaths
to mount on frosty front doors
and post above chimney mantelpieces
strewn with blinking lights.
Red holly berries
with their tiny black eyes
stare at us unblinking
watchfully waiting like Santa's elves
for Christmas to arrive.

Show n' Tell

My mind swims with thoughts of my grandmother
Nana who gave me the best present and gift
I ever received. I was nine that Christmas.
Taking my golden gyroscope from its blue box,
I spun it using a pull string and watched
it balance itself on the head of a dandelion
number-two led pencil without falling,
mocking gravity. Nana patiently listened
as I explained how it worked. Excited,
I took my present to school the next week
to show Miss Glavin and my fourth-grade class
the joy this "as-seen-on-TV" present
gave me. Other kids shared their favorite
presents, too: Mary proudly cradled her
Betsy Wetsy in her arms. Fred zoomed his
die-cast Tonka pickup truck back and forth
atop the teacher's front desk. And Sarah
played Elvis's "Hound Dog" with her Fisher
Price Kiddie Record Player. I recall
now how embarrassed I felt, thinking how
grand and extravagant their presents seemed
in contrast to mine. Even Miss Glavin
appeared to view my little gyroscope
as trivial. Back home from school I felt
ashamed and resentful. After a few
weeks I stopped playing with my gyroscope,
failing to realize that Nana's gilded
gift of attention never lost its value.

SEVEN

Septal Defects

We lived quaint lives of restraint–
until now.
Only three hours
since the bombing
we miss our home already.

Now in shelters, we remain
compliant untainted uncomplaining.
Trammeled tamped stamped
we know not what lies ahead
except the lies ahead.

We are the rubble crumble
the cramped encamped
the blood sampled
the cribbed crapped
the unscrubbed scraped
the scrapped scrupled
the hardscrabbled
the septic infected neglected
the disrespected
the rejected
the scared scarred
the poor.

Our sons and daughters
scribble quibble

John Sweeder

waddle waggle creep
whinny whine
sleep weep
play pray
and wonder
when their hearts will mend.

undocumented immigrant

a wave good-bye
a hug, a kiss
parentless
a thirsty Hispanic teen
travels north
on blazing train-car roofs
and searing dirt roads
away from king-pin violence
and cold fear
towards warm streets
paved of gold
caught crossing the border
an embarrassed patrol worker whispers to him
aquí está su casa billete de autobús

A Venezuelan Mother's Plight

Leaving my kids to work in swampy mines
I close my brown eyes and make my heart small.
My famished daughters are weak and show signs

of fever and ague. State-run headlines
claim the nation's economy won't stall.
Leaving my kids to work in swampy mines

I stand in vast watery pits—the kinds
that beget mosquitoes—and extract all
gold from pockmarked trenches with a vile brine

of chemicals. In jungle camp, my mind's
eye ricochets to my sound urban stall.
Leaving my kids to work in swampy mines

I reflect upon the number of times
I could not buy the proper pills for all
of my children, just painkillers. I pine

to see them again (and will in good time)
when I cash in the gold for my windfall.
Leaving my kids to work in swampy mines
I make my heart smaller, yet one more time.

Touch-Screen Viruses

Infected by the heroin
of propaganda wantonly
distributed by guileful
groomers, lone wolves hole up in dens
pecking and pawing at keyboards
and touch screens, exploring dark-web
corridors, in search of cut-rate
catalysts that'll help them pipe bomb
their way to immortality.
Strung out on power and praise, these
programmed predators patiently
pursue their soft-target prey, and
terrorize us as well: we, who
watch the carnage from our dens; we
media junkies who've become
addicted to viral strains of
violence and propaganda.

No Relief

police on beat
breach of peace
caprice

black boy
sixteen
concrete street
rap sheet
not unique

recoil
mistreat
extreme beat
blood cerise

press release
conversation piece
PC
cell phone
cover blown
disbelief

referee
justice of peace
wheels greased

UNTETHERED BALLOONS

case proceeds
disbelieve
repeat
never cease

no relief

Drones

When I was twelve years old, I enjoyed playing board games like Risk. In Risk, I tried to conquer the world – and so did my friend, Dwayne, who I used to compete against as we sat on the white concrete driveway behind our red brick row homes. Like military drones we hovered over a primary-colored, two-dimensional world that lay beneath us at ground-level. Dwayne and I took over countries one at a time by rolling sets of dice. Every outcome depended on chance. Whoever was lucky enough to roll the higher number conquered territories with make-believe armies. Whoever was unlucky got territories taken over. Continents fell to the victor. The game ended. No one was incinerated. No one was blown up. No one lost a son. No one lost a daughter. No one lost a loved one, like when I was twenty-one and thought I had to go to Viet Nam but didn't because I received a medical deferment. But Dwayne went to Viet Nam. He fought and died there. He had skin in the game.

Today, alone, seated comfortably in a cushioned chair with tablet computer on my lap, I watch YouTube videos of drones playing Risk overseas in the Middle East. But I don't have fun like I did when I watched the outcome of the dice in my driveway with Dwayne. Too many people have skin in the game, often young dark skin. Drones have no skin.

white noise

Listen to
the air conditioner's
fan whirring
the hard drive
re-booting
the plane with the banner-ad
farting above the beach
the politician's
whiny intonation
the muttered
sermon
the hissing
aerosol can
the cellphone
ringtone.

Listen closer to
the kiss on your forehead
as you awake
the engine's low rumble
just after you turn your wrist
the jingling of prodigal keys
you thought you lost
the tick-tock of
the grandmother's clock
the wooden mailbox lid

John Sweeder

as it shuts
the rhythm and blues
of Chuck Berry
the cork as it exits the neck
of your bottle of wine.

Closet Space

When Jean retired
from her job in the big city
she no longer needed
the keys to her corner office
and mahogany desk
and pigeon-gray file cabinet
where she kept dusty records
and confidential documents

She no longer needed
keys to her sun-roofed
SUV that transported her kids
each summer to Jersey beaches
where they wore neon pink and lime
swimsuits and played together
as a family in salty ocean surf
searching for seashells and sand crabs

She no longer needed
keys to her suburban
4-bathroom 4-bedroom home
with walk-in closets
where she raised her kids
in that perfect neighborhood
in that perfect school district
that her friends told her was "just perfect"

John Sweeder

She no longer needed
keys to her summer rental
home on the bay or the keys
to the 30-foot cabin cruiser she
used to drive to blue-water
offshore canyons to snorkel
and scuba or fish for bluefin tuna
in late August with her new boyfriend

She no longer needed
the key to her safe deposit box
where, decades ago, she
began putting aside money
for college educations
and wedding banquets
and retirement plans
and long-term health care
Today, she no longer needs
keys to her shed that once stored
her power mower and garden tools

She no longer needs
much closet space—
just a small condo
solo

Contextual

What color will you paint your bedroom?
Harbor gray? Egg-shell? Pale turquoise?
Is its color important?

What color is your skin?
Ghost white? Baby powder? Linen?
Is its color important?

What about her skin?
Coffee? Caramel? Cedar?
Is its color important?

What about your soul? What color is that?
Jasmine? Celestial blue? Seaweed?
Is its color important?

When is color important:
when you can choose it,
or when you cannot?

May-Day Mayflies

Esurient anglers lie in wait by
rocks along riverbanks where the hawthorn
blossoms bloom each spring. Mayflowers witness
hosts of dupable Mayflies emerge from
subaquatic schools of slime, rise above
water's surface to jazz in May's mid-air,
then sleep forever as their spawn return
to the river's lab of muck and mire.

Like the ephemeral May-day Mayfly's
spinning dance of death, spring-loaded scholars
graduate from schools like trout, are pursued
and swallowed by society's alpha
anglers, then digested into mainstream
society to consume and re-cycle.

Gothic Dreams

She dreamt in monochrome:
movies with curlicue plots,
dark heroes, darker villains
and guns that fired shots.

Movies with curlicue plots,
smoky potions, long shadows
and guns that fired shots
frightened her like electric current.

Smoky potions, long shadows,
high castellated walls and barred windows
frightened her like electric current
in a far-away underground laboratory.

High castellated walls and unlocked windows
transported her to a world once found
in a far-away underground laboratory,
but now exists mere feet from her home.

She's transported to a world once found
in silent movies, long before street-corner heroin,
but now exists mere feet from her home.
She dreams in monochrome.

presidential candidate

i am a straight-talking shoot-from-the-hip
compassionate conservative who holds
few progressive views no radical i
appeal to middle-class america
play to my base play bass guitar and blow
a mean saxophone thoroughly vetted
i possess an ivy-league law degree
am a true patriot having never
served in the military while fully
supporting our troops in harm's way god bless
them spot the tiny flag on my lapel?

media savvy i'm on facebook fox
cnn youtube msnbc
look directly into the camera
smile memorize my talking points pivot
like a point guard ignore opinion polls
know my opposition research blog tweet
text selfie my constituents daily.

i pledge to lower taxes invest in
infrastructure secure porous borders
provide paths to citizenship as the
climate changes increase our oil and gas
and solar and wind production outsource
fair trade to combat isis and social

security so our grandchildren can
play safely in streets with needed prison
reform and capital punishment not
beholding to wealthy corporations
i accept dark money of any shade.

Trinculo's Insight

Misery acquaints a man with strange bedfellows.
  –Shakespeare's *The Tempest II, ii, 40*

Like the stranded Renaissance Fool who sought
shelter beneath wretched Caliban's cloak
as the tempest bellowed at the Bermudas,
the urban shipwrecked student seeks relief
from the sweltering back-room pen strokes of
canary-yellow politicians who
veto tax increases for his schooling.

But when disgruntled citizen sailors
rise up to sing songs of injustice, and
uncloak political wheels that captain
ships of state, marooned body politic
begins to revive and the storm passes.

EIGHT

Faith

Faith is the wriggling eel
slipping through our fingers
when we feel lost.

… the magician's snake
popping out of its counterfeit can
surprising us.

… the pet ferret
awakening from "dead sleep"
clawing at us.

… the haloed phoenix
rising from its ashes
teaching us how to fly.

Faith is the paschal lamb
reminding us
of sacrifice and redemption.

Fortune of War

In Sidney, we listened to the Irish troubadour
strum her blonde guitar.

She sang Walker and Arnold's
"You Don't Know Me."

We sat shoulder to shoulder in the Fortune of War.
Two strangers, we were born hemispheres apart.

You savored your Jack Daniels.
You told personal tales of family and work: loving father

who had tended to your beloved children,
aged mother, and native brushwood fences.

The ambient music wept.

I strove to untangle the vernacular of your lament:
three months of waiting…three months
of battles…three months of war.

Like the minstrel who lifted her patrons' spirits,
I searched for the perfect, just-in-time words

that would uplift you—my accidental acquaintance—
but I could only offer you this belated soldier's prayer.

Give Me Retirement
(inspired by Walt Whitman's "Give Me the Splendid Sun")

Give me retirement with anytime wake-up mornings;
hours to read daily newspapers from home and abroad;
Give me sunlit living rooms with cathedral ceilings,
thin white curtains, warm coffee with cream;
Give me fig trees, yellow dahlias, red knockout roses;
Give me farmers' markets—slow-
paced—picking peaches and
cantaloupes, the smell of each one, ensuring its ripeness;
Give me salt air, salt water, small bay boats for fishing—
days with light ocean breezes;
Give me boardwalks with laughing children
wearing bright swimsuits.
Keep your cold, brutal Februarys with incessant north winds;
Keep your doctor's visits, abstruse prescription plans;
Keep your obituaries, your funerals (never forgetting those
you loved and those that loved you);
Keep your politicians, cynicism, lies.
Give me hopeful college students—
returning from classrooms each
summer to work and save;
Give me their late-night conversations about their futures—
their lovers, their lives;
"Their faces and eyes forever for me."

Light and Dark at the Cineplex

At noon on Tuesday Trish drives her vintage
red coupe to the local Cineplex. Seated

by herself in the 5th from the last row
of a darkened movie theater, she

removes the bag of unsalted popcorn,
purchased the day before, from her paisley

pocketbook, a treasured gift from her niece.
As Trish watches PG-rated coming

attractions, she noshes on her crackling
snack with mouth closed, but is distracted by

a small light source emanating from the
breast pocket of a gray-bearded man seated

arm-in-arm with an ombré-haired woman in
the row behind. Trish says to herself, *It's*

rude of him not to turn off his cell phone,
and then thinks, *But what if it's his daughter*

who's trying to reach him? Maybe she's caught
in a violent rain storm and needs rescue?

UNTETHERED BALLOONS

Trish refocuses her attention towards
the screen in front as the feature film begins.

Several minutes later she notices
other translucent particles of light

appearing as arrays of tiny shooting
stars falling from the blackened sky. Nonplused,

she tries to square this circle by imagining
how such a singularity occurs.

Like film itself, it is dreamlike. Trish deduces
these shooting shards of ephemera are mere

droplets of rain that have leached through the
roof of the aging movie theater and bent

the projector's light beams like a prism—
aqueous beads of stardust, the stuff of dreams.

Apparitions and Relics

Have you ever smelt an apparition?
It's redolent of two old leather boots,
or a sodden, mildewed grandfather's clock
that's left behind after a flood. Picture
muddied laces and toe moldings: wet earth
sleeping on soaked floors—sorrowful signals.

Fetors, molds, and muck are doleful signals
that help us remember. Apparitions
seldom stray far from their homes here on Earth.
Lost time travelers, unable to boot
their souls into Paradise, they picture
themselves as still pendulums—inert clocks.

Few things seem more useless than unwound clocks
that will no longer keep time. They signal
their hollowness, like monochrome pictures
of little boys' blank stares. Apparitions
don't *do*: they *suggest*. Their old clocks and boots
become relics once their spirits leave Earth.

We humans treasure these vestiges. Earth
stores them for us, as we carefully clock
their worth and former purpose. Antique boots
and old clocks are seeds of recall, signals
used to remind us that apparitions
aren't shifty-eyed portraits in framed pictures

who pursue humans as they pass. Pictures
of lost loved ones who once walked upon Earth
don't supplant relics of apparitions:
ears relish the tic-tocks and bongs of clocks.
Hands cradle well-worn footwear. They signal
time's run out for the departed. But boots

and clocks ignite our senses, ones that boot
memories into overdrive. Picture
yourself an apparition who signals
your loved ones after you depart from Earth.
What relics would you leave behind? A clock?
Boots? Photographs? Not all apparitions

think as apparitions should. Some leave boots,
others clocks. Scant few designate pictures.
While still on Earth, sagely choose your signals.

Winter's Clean-up
(in Memory of Alan Kepner)

Just like Bun-Bun, Bill's pet bunny rabbit,
I too noticed the ramshackle water
tower which, bent over like an old man
suffering from COPD, sat adjacent
to the soon-to-be auctioned-off farmhouse

where Bill lived with Alan, who was in hospice care.
I stared at Bill's white three-day-old stubble
that outlined his pink lips which, when he smiled,
revealed sixteen yellow crooked teeth.
I obeyed each of his final commands.

This eccentric lover sat on the floor,
legs crossed like a levitating swami, amongst
dried un-swept leaves blown in by winter's wind
through unattended windows and doors.
He barked: "Throw it out!" or "Give this away!"

I witnessed him slowly inventory
every closeted bedroom memory,
fingering each one lovingly as he removed
from wooden clothes hangers the herringbone
jackets and Oxford dress shirts they once wore

or the chrome art deco waffle iron
and red Kitchen Aid mixer that lay hidden

like two recluses, moribund for months,
behind the oaken cupboard pantry doors
of their almost-haunted farm house

where Bill and Alan cooked and ate and slept
in harmony (and discord, like their set
of unmatched dishes) off and on for years.

Our Father

We find him lying right-angled
on a concrete floor at the bottom
of cellar steps, semi-conscious, reeking
of co-mingled sweat, feces, and alcohol.
He insists we not call a hospital.

We dial 911. Two EMT's
arrive minutes later lifting him
onto a cold, metal gurney.

Later in the year, we wheel him
to a cancer ward. Clear plastic tubes tunnel
into his throat letting a noxious, yellow
liquid escape.
"Old boy, it's time to clean these."
We watch as the surgeon swiftly
slides each tube separately from Father's neck.
His horizontal body leaps a foot
off the bed as if he were being lobotomized
with a wet sponge and electric current.

Father does not protest. With heroic
irony, he mutters, "This is ridiculous."

More hospice time at home.
More tube feedings.
More blood loss.
More chemo and radiation.

UNTETHERED BALLOONS

Less strength.
Fewer complaints.

He returns to the hospital again—unconscious.
Blood infusions.
Hours pass.
We consult with doctors.
Decisions to make.
Decisions to make.
A decision to make.

A saintly nurse pulls us aside
and privately, lovingly, helps us
realize that more transfusions only
delay the inevitable. We enter
his room one last time. Naked, alone
atop the white-sheeted hospital bed, void
of covers, exposed, fetal as if in
a womb, he lays there, innocent. He sits up
once, opens his eyes widely for a
moment, and envisions something
with awe and fear. Then falling back, curls
up again. We say goodbye and cry.

At his viewing in the church, he lays in
a coffin bed, wearing his red and black flannelled shirt,
gray polyester pants, brown steel-toed work shoes.
His Phillies bucket-hat rests silently next to him,
just above his left shoulder.
We smell the incense and memorize it
as his funeral mass begins.

Melanoma

With maw big as a butcher's cleaver,
with teeth yellow as linoleum scum,
with tongue crimson as Satan's cape,
this malignant mongrel bit off
a hungry-man's portion of a right calf.

His Ashes

In early fall, after most tourists have left
the island

to return to offshore homes, we place his ashes
in a makeshift castle

we build with wet brown sand
at dead low tide.

Saltwater consumes this ephemeral fortress
in small-scale bites

as wave after wave rushes and retreats like piping plovers
feeding at ocean's edge.

The golden sun blinks at us from the clouds above.
Pale ghost crabs

audit our work from their burrows' breaches.
He did not think

there'd be many attendees at his interment
(and he was correct).

As his remains wash away with
comingled sand,

John Sweeder

we silently pray the *Our Father, Hail Mary,*
and *Glory Be,*

then collectively whisper, "Long live the king."

The Mathematics of Faith

Calculate how long you will live without
Googling it. Will you survive until you
reach eighty? You remember your parents
and siblings died when they were younger than
you are now. You look forward to dining
out with your spouse in expensive seafood
restaurants you haven't been to yet. You
allot time for physical exercise.
You must visit each one of your doctors
more often. At night you have dreams about
jobs you once held, and fret about why these
visions are so disquieting. You are
thankful for opportunities you have
to recite your poems publicly,
thankful for those who have inspired you,
thankful you are still productive— neither
stagnating nor despairing—having faith
your life adds up to something more than words.

Acknowledgements

My sincere thanks go to

Eva Feeley, creative writer, mensch and poetry advocate who believed in my work from the start and never gave me less than her unfailing support for my writing.

Marya Small Parral, my fellow poet and friend, who unselfishly critiques my writing with her caring and discerning eyes and keen intellect.

Maria Taney and my fellow writers from the Jersey Cape Writers who have responded to my poetry and prose with kind and gracious support.

Antoinette Libro, Emari DiGiorgio and the other talented poets who comprise the South Jersey Beach Bards and SJ Poets Collective. I thank them for affording me opportunities to share my poetry with wider audiences at the annual summer Beach Bards Poetry & Reading Series in Sea Isle City, NJ and at the monthly *World Above: Open Mic & Featured Reading* events in Atlantic City respectively.

John Sweeder

My long-time scholarly colleagues Francis Ryan, Brother Emery Mollenhauer F.S.C., Jim Butler, Jack Seydow, Claude Koch, John Keenan, Charles Kelly, Sidney MacLeod, Gerald Johnson, Maryanne Bednar, Carl Lefevre, Richard Newton and the other La Salle and Temple University faculty upon whose shoulders I stand.

List of Credits for Poems Previously Published

"The Drifters" originally appeared In *Adelaide Literary Award 2018 Poetry Anthology*, pp. 95-96. Adelaide Book, LLC. New York. Ed. by Stevan V. Nikolic.

"Wonderwheel Dreams" originally appeared in the *Opening Line Literary 'Zine,* June 2015, p. 15.

"Blues Busker," "Light and Dark at the Cineplex," and "His Ashes" originally appeared in *Adelaide Literary Magazine*, April 2018. Year III. Number 12 Issue. https://adelaidemagazine.org/p_jsweeder.html

"Floating in Place" originally appeared in the *Ocean City Sentinel,* May 29, 2014, p. A8.

"The Birder" originally appeared in *River Poets Journal, 2017— Special Edition "Windows,"* Vol.11, issue 1, p. 16.

"Sister Collette" originally appeared in the *Opening Line Literary 'Zine*, March 2015, p. 27.

"Perishing Twice" originally appeared the *Opening Line Literary 'Zine*, December 2014, p. 22.

"He Writes with his Actions" originally appeared in *The 2016 Poetry Marathon Anthology*, edited by Caitlin Jans, p. 43.

"Child Artist" originally appeared in the *Opening Line Literary 'Zine*, February 2015, p. 26.

"sudden buds appear" originally appeared the *Haiku Journal* (2016), Issue #46, n.p.

"wild backyard mint leaf" originally appeared in the *Haiku Journal* (2015), Issue #37, n.p.

"Beach-town Christmas" originally appeared in the *Ocean City Sentinel*, Wednesday, December 9, 2015, p. A8, and then the *Cape May County Herald*, December 19, 2018.

"Septal Defects" originally appeared in the *Opening Line Literary 'Zine*, November 2014, p. 29.

"undocumented immigrant" originally appeared in the *Burning-word Literary Journal*, January 2016, p. 27.

"Touch-Screen Viruses" originally appeared the *Opening Line Literary 'Zine*, Winter 2016, p. 23.

"Drones" originally appeared in *Shantih Journal*, Spring/Summer 2017, Issue 2.1.

"Mayday Mayflies" originally appeared in the *Opening Line Literary 'Zine*, May 2015, p. 17.

"Gothic Dreams" originally appeared in the *Opening Line Literary 'Zine,* June 2015, p. 14.

"presidential candidate" originally appeared the of *Opening Line Literary 'Zine,* Autumn 2015, p. 16.

"Trinculo's Insight" originally appeared in the *Opening Line Literary 'Zine,* April 2015, p. 16.

"Faith" originally appeared in *Ancient Paths Literary Magazine,* May 14, 2016, [online], *https://www.facebook.com/permalink. php?story_fbid=10153691181735958&id=124626725957&comment_tracking=%7B%22tn%22%3A%220%22%7D*

"The Mathematics of Faith" originally appeared in the *Opening Line Literary 'Zine,* July 2015, p. 20.

About the Author

A poet and memoirist, John Sweeder has had his work published in *Adelaide Literary Magazine, Burningword Literary Journal, Shantih, Haiku Journal, River Poets Journal, Ancient Paths Online,* and *The Opening Line Literary 'Zine,* among other venues such as *The Cape May County Herald, Ocean City Sentinel, The 2016 Poetry Marathon Anthology,* and *Dear Cancer… The Anthology (2015).* A Finalist of the Adelaide Literary Award for Poetry 2018 and Semi-finalist in in the 2019 Willow Run Poetry Book Award, John is listed in *Poets & Writers* Directory of Poet & Writers; has self-published *Breathing through a Straw: A Memoir for Baby Boomers and Neurotic Catholics* at https://jsweeder.wordpress.com/ as well as *Faith Genes for the Blue Jean Generation: A Self-help Memoir* at https://www.amazon.com/Faith-Genes-Blue-Jean-Generation-ebook/dp/B07BH84DY1 (2018).

Now retired from a 38-year career in in basic education in the field of English/Communication Education and in higher education as a teacher-educator, John worked twenty of those years as a Professor of Education for La Salle University in Philadelphia, Pennsylvania. While in academia, he published several scholarly articles, presented at national and international conferences, served as a conference research paper reviewer for the AACE (2006) and NECC (2004-2007), and won awards for SITE's Best Theory Paper (1997) and SITE's Best Use of Video in Teacher Education (1995). In addition, he co-authored an academic textbook issued by Peter Lang Publishing, Inc. entitled, *Drowning in the Clear Pool: Cultural Narcissism, Technology, and Character Education* (2002). John received his B.A. from La Salle College, his M.Ed. and Ed.D. from Temple University.

Having lived and worked most of his life in Yardley, PA and Philadelphia respectively, John now resides in Ocean City, New Jersey writing his memoirs and poetry and honing his skills as a back-bay saltwater angler. He is active in several poetry societies located in southern New Jersey; included among them are The Jersey Cape Beach Bards, the South Jersey Poets Collective, the Great Bay Artists and Poets, and the Jersey Cape Writers. He continues to present his poetry at a variety of open-mic events in Somers Point, Ocean City, Sea Isle City, and Atlantic City, NJ and has been the featured poet at the Bayshore Center's "Night of Revelry" in Port Norris, NJ. (2018) and at The Beach Bards Poetry & Prose Reading Series (2015, 2016). Most recently, John has had "A Moral Experiment or No Shades of Gray" published in the anthology, *By the Beautiful Sea: A Collection of Writings from the Jersey Cape* (2019).

www.ingramcontent.com/pod-product-compliance
Lightning Source LLC
Chambersburg PA
CBHW071419070526
44578CB00003B/618